90 DAYS

OF HELL JAIL

INSIDE OF

JAIL

TABLE OF CONTENTS

DEDICATION

This book is dedicated to all of my loved ones. I speak to you all as one, because the love is as real as it gets. I would like to begin with mentioning my brothers, who are no longer here with us. All of your legacies and impact are forever ingrained in me. I pray we all see each other at the highest level of paradise. I love you all, and I promise to strive to be better and continue to uphold your names in honor and constant supplication.

This book is also mainly dedicated to my brother and dear friend Cadaani. I love you bro. May Allah grant you the highest level of paradise. You'll never be forgotten. I remember my final call with you when I first got locked up. You told me I'd come out of this situation a better person. You believed in me when I had lost belief in myself. You were a genuine soul and that's how you'll always be remembered as. I'll continue to pray that we unite in the highest levels of paradise. You're forever in my supplications. I love you family.

To all my brothers behind those walls who are fighting every day for their freedom. I know it ain't easy in there dealing with the hardships of reality while knowing you are "out of sight, out of mind." My brothers, you all want a real shot at life, an opportunity to live right. Society has written all of you off as failures, but see, I have got to see the great people that are behind these walls. The disciplined & knowledgeable individuals that I've come across who

helped shape me to become a better person every day I was in there. Y'all know who you all are. My brothers, the voiceless. Y'all are who I do it for. It's forever FREE DA REAL.

Also, to my loved ones, dear friends, and dear family members, my people. Y'all never switched on me at my lowest and helped push me when I came home.

I know y'all don't boast about loyalty and being real, but I'm going to boast about all of you. You all know who you are. From the days in solitary, to phone restrictions.

From warning me about the dangers of the lifestyle, to constantly reminding me where that lifestyle has brought me. Whether it was giving me rides to the gym while I was on an ankle monitor, or advising my younger brothers while I was sent away. I'll also never forget how yall picked up every single jail call without making me feel like I was a burden. Always telling me there's more to life and how I got to think differently. All of you have been there on the good days and the darkest of days. You all were there for me & I love every single one of you for that.

You guys considered these " the little things," but the "little things" go a long way with me. I pray Allah blesses you with everything you all deserve in this life and the next. We're forever locked in! I love you all !

This next dedication is to my immediate family. All my siblings, from oldest to youngest, I love you all. Yall all have different ways of showing me love, but it's love. I put y'all through a lot over the years. You all had to deal with a different type of pain compared to most, but it's all up right now. To my Pops,

I got mad love for you no matter what. I wasn't leading by example before, but I'm ready to take on that role now. I love you all, and no words can compare to how much you all mean to me.

To my older brother Abdulahi, I'm praying that Allah restores your health in the best ways possible. I always imagined what life would look like if you had your health in full effect. I know I wasn't there during vital times of your life, but I'm here now. You've battled with autism your whole life, yet you shine with that smile no matter what the day offers. I love you bro. I pray that Allah keeps you blessed, and know your lil bro is here for you now. I'm not going anywhere this time. All our other siblings got your back and are there for you, and I got you as well big bro. Love you.

I also want to thank my beloved aunts, who have played a major role in my life. I consider all my aunts like a mom to me. I don't know anyone as strong as all of you. Y'all holding it down and it doesn't go unnoticed. This book is dedicated to all of you, thank you for never giving up on me, my dear aunties. Thank you for always having my mom's back, even when times get hard. I'll forever love you all for that.

This book would not have been possible without my Hooyo Macaan (Beloved Mother) . I'll never forget those difficult drives, having to go state to state to make it to my court dates. You have always been a hardworking mom, you're always putting your children's needs before your health, wealth,

and well-being. Your dedication and sacrifice is unmatched. I also want to highlight how you raised our brother Abdulahi. It is not an easy task to raise an autistic child, but you did it, with immense patience and pure love.

Hooyo, you were always there for me through the darkest of days and I am forever grateful for that. Hoyoo I want you to know that I love you from the depths of my heart. This book is a testament to your never-ending support and the unconditional love you have shown me. Thank you for being my rock, my guiding light, and my inspiration. I got you no matter what. I love you Hooyo.

Last but not least, this book nor anything I have accomplished, or will accomplish in life couldn't be attained without the grace and blessings of Allah. Alhamdulillah (All praise to Allah) for everything. I'm forever grateful and humble to be blessed with another shot at life.

JAIL INSIDE OF JAIL

It was a critical moment in a game of chess, a battle that mirrored the complexities of life itself. My king's safety was at stake, and I found myself contemplating the sacrifice of my rook to survive. Limited options left a nigga no choice but to consider sacrificing my bishop. Engaged in this mental battle with me was my Muslim brother, Ahki.

Chess became our refuge, a means to escape the harsh reality of our shackled existence. Chess was more than just a game; it was a metaphor for life, a training ground for my everyday life decisions. As I pondered whether sacrificing my bishop was the right move, I reminded myself never to underestimate my gut feeling, which I've failed to do for most of my life.

My gut was urging me to make this sacrifice, and so I did, waiting patiently for Ahki's response. His poker face had a level of respect, a silent acknowledgment of how far I had come as a chess player. Patience was my ally, guiding me to make decisions with a calm mind.

Ahki's next move held the power to shape the game's outcome. It could lead to a sacrificial sequence that would put me in check within the next two moves, or he might set up a trap to test my next move. In the game of life, thinking five steps ahead was crucial; failing to do so would blind me to what lay ahead.

As I contemplated the complexities of the chessboard, a gust of wind brushed past me, signaling the presence of a commotion. I'm not going lie, shit caught me off guard. Correctional officers in full raid gear stormed into the cell block, ready to wreak havoc in someone's cell. It was about to go down.

Suddenly, my inmate number was yelled out and heard all across the cell block. "766-361"! My heart skipped a beat as I hoped they hadn't somehow discovered my cell phone. I had kept it hidden from previous searches.

I hope these devils don't find it. My lil android was my only way to keep updated with the outside world. I wasn't on any social media platforms; I just used to educate myself on finding a different route in life. I felt like I failed in life. I wanted something different for myself, but the temptations of the fast lane were still there. Yet, there was no time to dwell on all that now. I shouted to Ahki, "This game isn't over yet brotha!" With a confident smirk, I knew that a dub was within reach. I made my way toward my cell, but my eyes widened in anger and frustration once I made it there.

The devils were tearing up my belongings, ripping everything into pieces, including my prayer rug and Quran. The sacredness of these items meant nothing to these devils. In an attempt to stop the devils from violating the remainder of my religious items and legal paperwork, I lost control & rushed towards them, and spazzed out. "Hey, that's my religious book! What the f*** are you all doing?" One of the officers charged at me and slammed me towards the cell wall, detaining me forcefully. I could hear the excitement in all their voices, "FOUND IT!"

The realization hit me like a punch to the gut. I was cooked. My major concern was that I was going to be cut off from communicating with the family, a communication that took me a long time to build up again. The devils' next step was to degrade me as a man by conducting a strip search, as they sought to ensure I had no weapons of any kind. In all reality, animals get treated with more respect. This method the devils used on us while incarcerated was similar to how enslaved people were treated.

The devils make sure to degrade you mentally, physically, and spiritually, & dealing with it for years has always fueled my frustration to higher levels. Amongst the devils was known as "Red Beard." His hatred towards me as a black Muslim man ran deep. The hatred from this devil stems all the way back from my very first day behind these walls. The day he found out I was Somali and Muslim, it bothered him. Why? I don't know. He always had a racist joke to make. I always laughed it off. I refused to show him any signs of frustration, but the devil pushed me to my limit on this day. Red Beard continued to tear apart my Quran while I was detained.

Acting like he was still searching for contraband but using that as an excuse to tear up my Quran. He was enjoying every moment of this. I looked at this devil with pure hatred, and he looked back at me with the same look. The devil had me shackled up and escorted me from my original cell to a place underneath the prison, known to us inmates as the dungeon. To think I'd be back here after a year of being out the way. After I spent 15 days here for a "fighting ticket", I promised I wouldn't return. Now look at me.

Here I am again. Back in the Dungeon. Solitary confinement. The Hole. Being in solitary is as if your sentence started all over again, from being yanked out of your original cell where you were comfortable and used to the environment.

I'll put it to you this way, imagine being in a cell as terrible as it is, but yet still having access to the limited basic human rights, such as buying commissary and catching up on your local newspaper, or just chopping it up with ya folks, through a 15-minute call. Now imagine having those little bits of freedom stripped away completely. Complete solitude. My freedom was taken away from me the day I became an inmate number, but when entering solitary, they take your mind as well.

What's crazy is how quickly life can switch up on you when incarcerated. Everything is liable to change within a day. I started the day with my usual routine, waking up, brushing my teeth, making wudu, and covering my toilet (since the toilet is in the cell & it's also jail etiquette, & respects the prayer). I woke up my cellmate for salaat and began the prayer.

Without prayer, I always felt lost within. A man with no connection with his lord is lost, and I was lost for years, but on this day, I felt my connection with the most high was getting back to where it hadn't been in a long time.

We finally made our way to the solitary block. Cell number 4 was my destination. Red beard unlocks the hell hole, throws me in there, spits on the floor, and yells, "Welcome to hell." I asked the devil, "How long do I have to be here?"

The devil laughs as he gets ready to lock the cell and yells, "I hope you die here, pirate." His words repeated constantly in my head, and for the first time, the words of the devil truly got to me.

I snapped. In an attempt to punch him, he slams the cell door in my face, and I fall back into the cell's darkness. As Red Beard walks away, all I hear is his devilish laugh echoing throughout the solitary block.

Now all to my thoughts and my lonesome in this confined cell, I lay on this uncomfortable metal bed. I sat there in the darkness. I couldn't help but feel a surge of fear and uncertainty.

At that moment, my life flashed before my eyes. I thought to myself, how did I end up here? I started to reminisce about a younger KY, when life was simple, playing basketball and spending time with my loved ones, but reality kicked in....

All I saw was darkness and an uncertain future. As I thought of how long I'd be in this confinement, I truly felt I had entered hell. this was day one of jail inside of jail.

CONFUSION

As I slowly awaken in the darkness of my cell, a wave of unpleasant odors smacks my senses. I try to get myself back to sleep, hoping to escape the harsh reality of my situation. However, the discomfort of the metal bed I'm lying on, the back pains, and the chilling coldness, should make anyone realize how sleep is an elusive luxury.

I rose from the bed, feeling the aching in my muscles. I stumble towards the sink, hoping to quench my thirst. With a flick of the handle, I'm waiting for the sounds of flowing water, but instead, all I hear is the sputtering and coughing of the pipes.

A stream of brown, murky water sprays out, shit had me tight. Disgust and frustration boil up inside me. I was hella dehydrated, yet I still couldn't drink this tainted water. I was heated.

I turned off the sink and began pacing back and forth in my cramped cell, lost in deep thought. I find myself questioning the nature of my existence in this cell. When will I find out how long I got in this hell hole? As if in response to my silent plea, the jingling of keys reaches my ears from a neighboring cell.

My heart races with anticipation, and I rush towards the cell door, positioning myself underneath to maximize my chances of hearing and being heard.

Desperate, I yell, "HEYYYYY, C.O! How long do I have to be here?

HEYYYYYY! I know you hear me!" A voice responds, annoyed, but answering, "Shut up, I hear you!

17

You are currently under investigation. The institution can take up to 30 days to decide whether you'll be transferred to another maximum-security prison or remain in solitary confinement. So get comfortable Inmate, because you'll stay here for a while." I was sunt. How does any of this make sense?

They can't be doing this. Ramadan, a sacred month of fasting, will begin, and here I am, trapped in this dungeon. Will I have the opportunity to get out before Ramadan starts? If I'm here longer than expected, should I attempt to fast while confined in this unbearable environment? The thought of fasting becomes problematic, for I am already experiencing hunger and dehydration in this cell.

Even though, as a Muslim, fasting during Ramadan is mandatory. My situation had taken entirely over the principles and pillars of my faith. My stomach rumbles in hunger, reminding me of its empty state. The pain intensifies, intertwining with the overwhelming confusion swirling within my mind. Every possible scenario of the unknowns and injustices that await me plays out within my thoughts.

One part of my mind tries to reassure me, whispering that it will only be a few more days until I escape this suffocating box. The other part screams to lose all hope, letting it be known that I'm not going anywhere, especially any time soon.

ANGER

The throbbing vein on my forehead was a visual of the anger that had consumed me. The pounding headache I was dealing with surpassed any I had experienced in a long time. Yesterday, I was confused and stressed out. This led to igniting a fire of resentment within me.

I found myself trapped in this suffocating, narrow confinement, pacing back and forth, my anger escalating with each step. It reached a boiling point, and I couldn't contain it any longer. I yelled out from beneath the heavy metal door, desperate for answers, "C.O.!

When will I be out of this fucking place? Get me out of here!" My voice echoed from underneath the cold cell door, but there was no immediate response. I continued to pace around, mad as hell. Finally, the jangling sound of keys grew louder, drawing closer to my cell. This particular correctional officer was unfamiliar to me, appearing as though he could easily be mistaken for an NBA player.

His expression was unreadable, a poker face that spoke volumes. Before he could walk past the cell, I shouted, "C.O.! How long do I have to be here?" He continued to approach, his footsteps echoing in the narrow space. As an inmate, you become adept at discerning the different types of correctional officers you encounter. There are three main categories.

First, there are the "dickhead" officers who take pleasure in harassing and belittling us and letting us know we're nothing more than inmates, making it clear that they consider themselves superior. I often speculated that these officers carried their own insecurities and unresolved issues from their past.

Perhaps they were punked & mistreated themselves, and now they unleashed their frustrations on those already trapped in a living hell. The Second type of correctional officer wants to complete their shifts without any disturbances. Throughout my time behind these walls, I learned to deal with these two types of C.O's, even the "dickhead" all because of one reason, they both stay the same.

Every shift, you get what you see. Lastly, there is the third type and the worst of them all. These devils would wear a friendly smile during visitation, speaking kindly to my family, assuring them of my greatness, and even expressing hopes for my eventual release.

Yet, the next day, they would reveal their true colors, spreading hatred and reminding me of their contempt for my existence. The keys jangling ended as the C.O. stopped in front of my cell.

The weight of his presence hung in the air as I awaited his response, my anger barely contained. And then he uttered the words that shattered any hope I had left. "They have you under investigation, so sit tight, bud. You're going to be down here for a while." My frustration peaked as I continued pacing back and forth.

I stepped back and took off on the cell door in a rage. The impact got to my hand, leaving behind a bruised and swollen fist. Little did I know that this would be the first of many punches thrown at these walls throughout my time in this hell hole. Every time I swung, it was an outlet for the built-up anger that consumed me.

DOG FOOD

Let me paint you a picture that captures the so-called "food" served to us in the penitentiary. Imagine chewing a piece of ground beef and grinding it down until it becomes unrecognizable. Now envision spitting that mixture right back onto your plate. Nine times out of ten, you wouldn't even consider eating or looking its way.

That's what the everyday meals looked like in solitary confinement, though I must clarify that it wasn't much different from the regular prison trays, which was bs itself. When I first got booked, I noticed a common misconception among people from the outside world that incarcerated individuals have access to a constant supply of commissaries such as ramen noodles and honey buns. Having such items is considered a privilege, not a right.

You must pay for them through the commissary to obtain them, but when confined, you lose access to these purchases. They leave niggas no choice but to rely solely on the three meager meals provided at specific times throughout the day. They'd slide trays through the slot starting at 6:00 am. Breakfast arrived as a single slice of bread, accompanied by some brown apple slices and a serving of cold grits.

The second meal of the day was a mixture of beans and some nasty sloppy joe for lunch. It's worth noting that lunchtime was considered the most disappointing meal of the day. As for dinner, it was served at 4 o'clock, and depending on the day, you might find a slice of bread alongside the same underwhelming sloppy joes, essentially providing no real variety or improvement from the earlier meal.

The time between dinner and the next day's breakfast felt excruciatingly long, a seemingly endless stretch of twelve hours during which we were expected to contain our hunger, having already struggled to consume the bullshit put on our trays.

I was taught never to stay comfortable because everything can change at the flip of a switch. One day, you might have the means to purchase items from the commissary store to the next store day being on commissary restriction. It's the pen. Shit is always liable to switch up. I wondered if animals such as dogs and pigs would even eat the food served on this metal tray.

Would a dog spit this food out? For a while, I called this shit dog food, but would a dog even lay his eyes on this? Who knows? One thing is for sure, a dog's meal for the day would contain my hunger better compared to this.

PACING NONSTOP

Living in solitary confinement revolves around one constant activity: pacing back and forth. However, pacing frequency differs in general population vs. solitary confinement. Even in max security, you can engage in activities and follow a routine and schedule. You could spend one part of the day playing chess with the homies, then the next moment bumping some tracks on your lil MP3 player, followed by a workout session, and cap off with a phone call to the fams. But in solitary confinement, I couldn't fully stretch my arms, and both hands could reach each side of the narrow walls.

The space was incredibly tight, and I knew the longer I stayed there, the more suffocated and claustrophobic I would feel. As I wake up from the cold metal bed, my first destination is the contaminated sink. Its surface is covered in dead roaches, and the paint peels off. Carmex or any lip balm is a luxury that doesn't exist in solitary confinement. So I developed a habit of constantly licking my lips as I paced back and forth, hoping it would help with the dehydration and soothe my crusty lips. Little did I realize that this habit was making shit worse.

Standing in front of the sink, a nigga desperate for some water. I'm dehydrated beyond explanation, and I know water is essential for my survival. I turn on the faucet, and to my relief, cold water immediately flows out. I drink and drink, feeling like I have discovered a well of ZamZam in a drought. (Zam Zam water is a sacred type of water found in the city of Mecca, Saudi Arabia) After days without proper hydration, the sensation is unparalleled. I drink straight from the sink, resembling a dog lapping water from a bowl.

Without cups or containers, this is my only option. But as I continue drinking, the taste slowly changes. What was once cold and refreshing tap water transforms into a sour, bitter flavor. I quickly spit out the water, pissed off by its taste and even more pissed by its brownish color.

I resumed pacing back and forth in my cramped cell. The water went bad, the food was terrible, and my back pain intensified daily. The metal bed I sleep on offers no comfort or relief. As I continue pacing in this congested hellhole, my mind slips into deep thought. It's a mental pace, a constant comparison between my current surroundings and the life I had known before.

I draw parallels between this rusty prison sink and the clean, shiny sink in a luxurious Hilton hotel I used to vibe at after running plays. This was just another reminder of the fast-paced life I was once accustomed to.

I compare the cold, unforgiving metal slab that serves as my bed to the soft, plush mattress I used to sink into after a day of running up a bag. This constant pacing is not only physical but also mental. Days go by, and it begins to take a toll on my mental health in unimaginable ways.

Eventually, I stop pacing within my confinement and sit on the cold metal bed. My lips are beyond dried up, and I have never used the sink for drinking water since it went brown. At this point, the effects of dehydration were starting to impact me in ways I couldn't have imagined.

I got up & drank the brown water in pure disgust. It hit me that this may be the beginning of the end, but I have no idea what the future might look like. So, I got up and continued doing the only thing I knew how to do, pace nonstop.

ADVERSITY STRIKES! CAN YOU HANDLE THE CONSEQUENCES ?

I wake up to a thunderous slam at my door. It sounded almost as if an explosion happened right in front of my cell's door. "BANG BANG BANG" The slams to the door continue. I quickly rush off my metal bed and run straight to the door.

I didn't know what time it was, but it had to be no earlier than sunrise because I had yet to receive my breakfast tray. So as I look through the trey slot, I come across the correctional officer that brought me into this hell hole. C.O. Red Beard, a.k.a. the biggest devil the institution had.

"Cuff up inmate," The sergeant needs to see you in his office right now." You might be going back into gen pop." As soon as the devil uttered those words, I knew it was a lie. There's no such thing as an inmate who does less than 30 days in solitary for getting caught with a phone.

Unless they turn rat, that is, and to do something like that is a violation of everything I stand for. I've always been a firm believer that your losses are your losses. As a man, you gotta take it upon the chin to deal with whatever circumstances you find yourself in. You shouldn't point any fingers.

That's an act of cowardness and something no man should live by. So on the way to the sergeant's office, I'm chained from my legs to my hands. They always do this when transported from building to building for security purposes.

I walked through the cell block and saw one of my close homies yelling from his cell to get my attention. I was shocked, wondering what happened for him to be in solitary, and as I continued to walk past every cell, I saw a bunch of my homies being detained.

It was weird because all of us were Muslim. So it made me wonder, is the institution targeting all Muslims? Why is everyone in solitary? What's going on within the institution? Is this targeting, and why are these chains on my body getting heavier every step a nigga takes? It was pissing me off. I continued walking like a penguin. I started to think from the last time I was in this form of shackles.

A flashback of my last visitation years ago from my mother. They shackled me before visitation for security purposes. This day was one I'd never forget, and it was the first time in my life that I couldn't look my mother in the face. I wouldn't say I liked the concept of visits.

They were always a firm reminder that at the end of the 30 minutes, I'd be thrown right back to my cell and my mom back into the real world, but what's crazy is that wasn't the part that mentally messed me up.

It was the fact my mom had to see me at all-time lows, for her to see me shackled up and addressed by a number instead of my birth name, and top of all that, for her to converse with her son through a glass window truly puts you through a whole different type of pain.

My mind felt like a bullet wouldn't be as equivalent to this. I started seeing rays of sunlight on our pathway. My eyes couldn't handle the light, and my body couldn't handle the pressure and weight of the shackles pinching and applying pressure to every step I took. I felt as if the cuffs were getting ready to rip off my hands and feet. "HEY, C.O.!!!"

"Aye, man, loosen up these cuffs. Man, my hands are losing circulation. You big tweaking!" The devil smiled in a grimacing way. Before he began to speak, he took a long breath, a long breath that wreaked havoc on my nostrils.

The smell of this devil's breath was beyond tolerable. "INMATE, shut the FUCK UP! I didn't tell you to be a criminal, that's what you chose, and I'll be darn to give you any special treatment. So enjoy those cuffs because, unless you want them tighter, they're not coming off".

We finally make it to the sergeant's office, where my ticket will be read. In prison, a sergeant is basically above a correctional officer, and a captain and lieutenant are above them both.

Sergeants determine everything from behavioral discipline to prison transfers and also can recommend your security level to be raised. So, as we enter the door, I see two higher- ranked sergeants having a conversation drinking coffee and chewing dip (chewing tobacco).

I've seen this devil once on the compound, and the thing about this devil is he's one of those where you don't know what they're thinking. He stays poised with a poker face, so it's hard to determine whether he's walking around the compound on a mission to make your life hell. I firmly believed in never trusting these folks from the day my freedom was taken away.

So as always, I considered him like the rest of them, a devil. "INMATE 692778... Johnson". The guy before me in line was up next to speak with the sergeant. Within ten minutes of him being in the devil's office, I heard him cursing and screaming at the poker-faced devil."Sixty days!

60 fucking days! I didn't do shit! It wasn't my knife! It wasn't MINE !!! The sergeant stared at him casually without a care in the world. "He continued his frustration and rage as they dragged him back towards his cell.

I was up next. The questions rushed through my head in a swoop. How many days will I do in hell? Will the sergeant show any form of kindness to this situation?

It's not like I got caught fighting or got caught with a knife like the last guy. Will God show mercy on me? I haven't prayed in 12 days. Will he punish me? Nah, he's punished me enough for a lifetime.

The arrogance within continued on in my head. I think 20 days is the max they can give me. Or is it? I've seen folks get shipped to another prison and get a security level raise without solitary time. What if they don't find me guilty, so I should be good? I know I'm good.

"AHMED 766-361, come into the office." As I penguin walked my shackled body into his office. I saw three devils sitting right by the sergeant. The office felt good, almost as if it was the only place in the prison that didn't smell like animal waste, and it had air conditioning.

One more devil slowly enters the room and closes the door behind me. To no surprise, it was Red Beard. He let his presence be known and read my ticket out loud for all to hear. "Inmate 766-361 has been on my radar for months, "he's always been very discreet whenever we've conducted cell raids.

"It was also reported that the inmate was seen numerous times for having a light beaming from his cell unit". We believe he was using this phone to make deals of some kind, which is a major security breach." That's all the major parts of our findings with this inmate Serg.". Red Beard smiled as if he won an Oscar for reading that out to the Serg.

It felt like I was on trial in a courtroom, but I was already in jail. The only main difference between a courtroom and here is I felt all odds were against me, with no lawyer. I was my representation. I started to wonder in deep thought. Is this poker-faced sergeant a man of ration? Or is he just like the four devils in the room?

The Serg. continued to stay silent, and this started to frustrate me. That's when I spoke my mind. "Hey, Serg. I've already spent 12 days here without any word on how much longer I gotta sit in here, so I don't care what all of you do. Just get this over with." My out date ain't changing regardless, so do what you do".

This mentality of "my out date ain't changing" was a universal law shared by many inmates behind bars. A lot of us carry the mindset that they can put us in solitary and harass us and confiscate state property all they want, but they can never stop that release date.

I spoke my peace as I waited for the Serg. to respond. I was shocked. The poker-faced devil burst out in laughter and continued on and on. "HAAAAAAAA HAAAAAAA, "Ok, your out date ain't changing, huh you're serving three and a half years, so ya, you're right on that."

"Unfortunately, you're right. We can't change that. We're not the courts, Haaaaa hah haaa." What I can do for you is this. I can give you an out date for your solitary with time credited for the 12 days you've already served". A feeling of relief was printed all over my face.

Finally, I thought to myself, these past 12 days have been nothing but confusing. Red Beard stares at me and starts to grin. "So when's my out date Serg"? Silence took over the room. "Inmate 766-361, I find you guilty of having a cellular device which is a major security breach.

I recommend that your security level be raised and that you get sent off to another maximum-security prison. Until your ride- out date, you will be serving an additional 78 days in solitary with your current 12 days credited". I was outraged! "90 days!"

"Are you crazy" y'all can't do that" Y'ALL CAN'T DO THAT." I was furious and filled with rage. "90 days"! All the devils in the room continued to smile as the devil who brought me there pulled my shackles as directed my way back into hell. 90 days. For 90 days, I can't call Hoyoo (mom) or check up on my autistic brother & see how the rest of my family is doing. I was tight. On my way out, I yelled to the devil,

"Can I make a phone call & call my family"? Red Beard yelled back, "Should have made all the calls you needed on that phone we found, Inmate. "Your family will hear from you in 90 days. "What happened, Mr. Tough Guy? I thought you were ready to live with the results?"

On my walk back into hell, I started to think to myself. Can I truly live with the results? Am I ready for the adversity that awaits me? My thought process started to go downhill as I passed more confinement cells.

Truly I am a failure in life. I'm a young man who didn't go to college and hasn't made his mom proud or given her anything to smile about. Then I wondered what this lifestyle had brought me. When will I let it entirely go? Questions and life scenarios filled up my head. It all came to a stop. My walk ended, and the doors to hell were unlocked once again.

This time, it felt different. A bright day wasn't in my cards. I sat on the metal bed and stared at the wall questioning life. With all the bs weighing on my shoulders, can I live with the results... & to be honest... I don't think so....

RESENTMENT, RAGE & BITTERNESS

I sat on my metal rack, staring into the darkness in rage and resentment. My hands were covered up with blood and bruises. My body and face were drenched in sweat, and my arms throbbed with unbearable pain. I've been running on no sleep since the night the devil gave me my solitary confinement sentence, 90 days in hell.

The throbbing of my fists continued, and I knew laying down wouldn't change anything to help soothe the pain. So I continued to do what was numbing the pain all night, and in a sense, this was numbing my mind as well.

I stood up facing the cell door and took a full swing back, and started connecting haymakers at the cell door. Punch after punch after punch. I felt I could not let up. The devil passed by my cell door after hearing all the punches. "Inmate, SHUT THE F*** up"! As I listened to his keys jangling past my cell, I continued to punch even harder.

I started seeing much more blood pouring from my knuckles as I struck at the steel door. " AHHHHHHHH! I promise I'm not going to stop" !!! Y'all think y'all going to get away with this. I swear to god I'll make y'all life hell for as long as y'all have me in here" AHHHHHH !" I threw more haymakers at the wall. " AAAHHH" now I switched to stomping the cell door.

"AHHHHHHHH! " I was outraged with resentment towards a system that had detained me in this small confinement. The feeling of letting up started to weigh on me, but I kept on ignoring the feeling. I was throwing punches at a faster rate than before.

The blood on my fists started dripping off my nails. I changed my aim towards the sink. Now, that's it! I thought, I'll just kick this sink in and flood my cell to piss off the correctional officers.

Once they see water flooding from outside my cell, that'll piss them off. "HEY, INMATE !! STOP RIGHT NOW, OR WE WILL MACE YOUR CELL. THIS IS YOUR FINAL WARNING, D*** HEAD".

I immediately calmed down. I had never been maced before, but with the unbearable pain I caused upon my fists, & if they did spray the mace, it would amplify the pain even more and burn my hands off.

I paced back and forth within my confinement and stared at my hands. Blood drenched and bruised up. I couldn't even extend my fingers. My middle finger would barely move above the halfway mark. I sat on my metal bed in deep thought and reflected on my current predicament.

As of late, all I've been feeling is rage, hatred, and resentment towards everything & everyone. I hated my life and what it's become. I hated the corrections system for allowing me to see incarceration. I resented all those who crossed me and left me for dead over the years.

I honestly reached a point of true bitterness. I thought I had gotten over this mental warfare during my early stages of incarceration. I thought I'd never experience this bitter stage again, but here I was, once again... I hadn't reached a low point where I even hated myself, but the hate was directed toward my individual failures instead.

I started to believe this was Allah's punishment for all my life's mistakes, & that this was just the beginning. The countless nights of sleepless hours I subjected my mom to, were a constant source of guilt and regret. For the past 15 days, I was back to being disconnected from my lord. I used to pray five times a day for this disconnect not to happen again.

I led a lifestyle where prayer was undermined and where you view yourself as if you're untouchable. Now instead of worshiping the most high during my time in this hell hole, I'm sitting on this metal bed, falling for the devil's bait. I'm staring into the bruises and cuts of my damaged fists as I stand up in resentment, bitterness, and rage, ready to continue this onslaught on my cell door once again.

THE GUEST, THE PEST & THE BURDEN

The noises continued   I twisted and turned and went in and out of sleep rapidly. The metal bed wasn't doing me any justice whatsoever. I continued to twist and turn, and finally the rattled noises concluded. I slowly closed my eyes, ready to enter a deep sleep, but the noises started to continue. My eyes slowly rolled back open to see this furry creature looking me dead in the eyes. I jumped up in complete shock. "WTFFFF"...

I yelled in shock. The creature continued staring me right in the eyes, unhinged, as he sat on the edge of my bed, face to face. It's like he told me to wake up and start my day. I jumped up, turned on the sink, and cupped my hands to splash water at this creature. I immediately splashed water all over my bed as I chased this creature away. I was still in shock from being awakened by this creature. I wondered if this was real or just a bad dream. Then reality hit, and my everyday existence was a bad dream.

It ran faster than anything I've ever seen. You'd think you saw the flash in rodent form. As a youngin, I had seen my fair share of mice, but I've never seen a rat that's equivalent to the size of my two fists held together. So as I stand on top of my sink, I see my small confined cell from a higher view.

I looked around at every angle and every corner of the cell, trying to figure out where in the hell did master splinter go? As a matter of fact, where did he even come from? Does he have a family? When will he return, because when he does, I'm posted.

This cell will only shelter one of us, and that's me. I saw the coast was clear, and my rodent foe was nowhere to be found. Common traits of a rat, I thought to myself, when the pressure heats up, they definitely know how to exit the kitchen.

I'm scouting out the entire cell, and there's really not much to look at besides under the bed or the corners of the toilet. Nothing in sight. I lay down hoping to find some rest. I was sleep deprived and stressed. A comparison can be made to a meth addict who's been up for days. I twisted and turned on this metal bed, trying to find comfort.

Whenever I slept on my back, I experienced back pains, so I'd always end up sleeping on my sides, which was exactly where my focus was on. I'm dozing in and out of sleep. Hopefully, I have a dream or even get a small visual of me reunited with my loved ones. I started thinking of my baby sister and how she thinks I'm in out of town college for the next four years.

Does she believe that? I knew I had failed her as a brother. I closed my eyes and completely disregarded my failures, & the conditions I'm living in. I miss you sis. I reached for my sister's hand, "Sis!!!" I missed you." She stood silent, smiling, playing with my hands.

Sis, I miss you. Silently she grabbed her eraser and set it on the palm of my hands, and smiled. I stared at the eraser for a while and smiled, sometimes I wished I could use the eraser in my hands and erase my whole life and start over. Starting with being a great older brother to my sister and being present for her.

I smiled at her again and held the eraser. It started to move. I looked at my sister, wondering if she knew why the eraser was moving...... silence in the air. My baby sister faded off into the darkness. When I woke up, my baby sister was nowhere to be found. I still had the moving eraser in my hands. I opened my eyes & I was shook. In disbelief of what I just had seen, I kept on shaking that crawling feeling off my hand .

Ain't no way. The roach squirmed out and ran off like an Olympic gold medalist. I immediately rushed to the sink to wash my contaminated hands. I tried to process everything. This roach was the size of a thumb. The roaches I'm used to seeing are much smaller and only come out at night. This roach was their ancestor and had had no curfew nor mannerisms.

I remember as a kid, when the small roaches would appear, they'd only act up amongst the household, but never when guests came around. I remember one time a whole bunch of family members came into town for a wedding.

I was probably around 8 or 9, but I remember everyone was vibing in the living room. I'm giving everyone hugs and greetings, but there he was, that one roach who popped out to enjoy the family reunion. See, the other roaches understood the plot, stay away.

This is a family function only, but you see, this specific roach was on one. The night before, he had a little too much RAID (bug spray) for his own good, and then pulled up trying to ruin a family reunion. Eventually, he ran off before any of the family spotted him out. When I look back, I can say the small roach was harmless compared to the beast I was living with. C.O: "TRAYS"

... "TRAYS". "TRAYS". It was time for us to eat.

The correction officer opened my cell door tray slot and slid my food toward the floor. Some of the sloppy joe fell off the tray. I wondered. This might be the best way to trap and kill the rat and roach and also see if there are more of their homies within my cell. I grab my tray and spill the sloppy joe all over the floor. I felt like a scientist conducting a series of experiments. I grabbed an empty bottle I found in my cell. I took the cap, and put some sloppy joe in there as a trap.

I also spread the remainder of the trey on the floor. I stood on the toilet seat and observed my cell floor from above in silence. Not even 10 minutes in, Master splinter appears from underneath my bed. I patiently continued to observe as I watched the beast playing with the sloppy joe.

Minutes later, three roaches dive in for their portion of the meal. It's a party in my cell, and I had no invite. A secondary rat runs from underneath my bed as well. He saw Master Splinter claiming his throne alongside the 3 roachkateers and didn't want any part of that. He stopped across from my water bottle trap, analyzed it, and ran away.

He probably looked at my trap as a joke. One of the roaches separated from his two brothers and ran to the other side, where Master Splinter was eating. This roach had to be the leader of his group because he felt the sloppy Joe was theirs for the taking and I can tell it didn't sit right with him seeing that a rat was eating good.

I continue standing still on my toilet like I'm the Statue of liberty, not moving a muscle or over breathing. I'm fully aware that the situation is heating up, and shit could pop off at any given moment. Both Splinter and Roach have reached a major boiling point as they face off. ...

The fight begins... and all I'm missing is popcorn for the main event. The intensity of the fight escalates as they twist and turn on the sloppy Joe. I looked to the other side and to my surprise the two other roaches were not paying attention to their homies' fight.

The sloppy joe they were swimming in had their full undivided attention, as their homie's battle wasn't a concern to them at all. I continued watching the main event from the top-floor view of my cell's toilet. That's where it hit me, I've been saying the words "my cell," but in all reality, I was just a guest within this confinement.

A guest living with a pest who will crawl into your palms with plans of taking over by any means necessary, but he'll never be able to achieve that because of the burden whose main objective is to gain your trust, all to then find the exit when things heat up.

You see, growing up, we were always taught to make our guests feel like they were at home, give them comfort and let them feel like they belong, and that's exactly what I did for myself as I leaped from my statue pose down onto the pests and the burdens, creating havoc for them all. My time as a guest has finally come to an end. It's time a nigga makes himself feel at home.

STATE PROPERTY

"YOOO, FAMILY! YOOOOO FAMILY" KY! YOOOO. Who is in CELL 4? YOOOO" KY, YOU IN THERE! WAKE UP MY NIGGA". I woke up sweating bullets. The heat wave started to kick in the past couple of days. The thing about the institution is when it snowed, it felt like it snowed inside, and when it was hot, you had brothers sitting still to stay somewhat cool.

Today was no different. Sometimes shit would have me thinking about whether or not the temperature outside felt better than this. This wasn't it. I started to stretch and try to knock out a couple of pushups. I was hella tired from not eating any food. Especially in the past couple of weeks, hunger was taking its toll. I opened my legal paperwork and found the four slices of bread I put up for the past couple of days.

By adding some water to stretch the bread, I'd be content, compared to only eating the slices by themselves. I opened my sink and started drinking out the faucet, I don't know why, but it felt like the more I drank it, the more dehydrated a nigga got. "KY" YOOOO" KY. "Someone calling my name?

I went towards the cell door and started to yell back from underneath the door. "Yoooo wassup who's calling my name". Unknown: "Man, you finally up nigga, don't tell me for over the past three weeks yo a** been slumped." "Ain't no way!" I recognized that voice from a mile away.

"Ahkiiiii wassup bro as salaam alaikum." 'What the hell these devils got you down here for bro"?

Ahki: "KY man, these mf tripping bro they done maced me tore up my Quran and legal paperwork, they tweaking hard ahki."

"Damn, bro, they did my Quran the same way," but they ain't mess with my legal paperwork, wallahi we gotta fight this."

Ahki:" Fight this?!"

Man ain't no winning vs. these shaytans man, and you should know this shit by now." "We never win with these folks. To them, we are just another number & state property.

They brought down 15 other Muslim brothers down here too. "I can't say too much, but I'll be sliding a note of everything going on since you've been here. KY, you are not going to believe this shit. It's been wicked on the compound".

I started to hear the loss of hope in Ahki's tone, which I was not accustomed to. He's always been very uplifting. Even though he's serving a life sentence, he's always been the type to keep his head above water. On top of all that, why are they bringing more Muslims down to solitary ?? The shit wasn't adding up.

"Keep yo head up Ahki, I yelled back, im a holla at you in a minute. Ahki: yup, fosho man. Also, by the way, you have a Quran in your cell?" "Nah, Ahki, they tore up my only one. We need to get the Imam down here asap. They hate letting him come down here. You know this warden got it out for a nigga."

Ahki: Ok, brother, I'll holler at you. Make sure you pray you're five salaats too. That's the only thing we can control here" And brother, it's the last three days of Ramadan, so let's take advantage." "Salaama alaikum" As I stood up from the door, I paced back and forth. Damn, they do have niggas in here as state property. I continued to pace back and forth. The more I walked, the more I was sweating. I sat down to cool off.

"Damn, it's Ramadan, and a nigga ain't fasting? This has to be why Allah is punishing me. Is this the reason I'm being punished? "On a real note, why fast if I ain't even praying." This mentality was one I was always warned about throughout my incarceration then.

I remembered Ahks words from the past. Ahki: "A Muslim who doesn't pray is equivalent to a non-Muslim." I knew when he told me this that I was far from perfect, and that fact hasn't changed today. Then I wondered what was making me scared to connect with my lord.

It was like every time I wanted to get close to my maker, the devil had his hold on me. I paced back and forth and picked up my legal paperwork. I flipped through, and to my surprise, I found a page from my ripped Quran. I looked at it briefly, but my heart wasn't in it. As I said, the devil had his hold on me, and all I wanted was to start problems with the corrections system.

They got all my brothers in this hell hole, and all for what? A note with a string attached slides through my door. I untied the sting off the paper and read the note. "From Ahki, "aye KY salaam aleikum. "Listen, bro, I know you are telling me to stay positive Ahki, but they brought down 15 of our muslim brothers. It got me tight bro.

They are trying to do us all wrong assuming the Muslims have been involved in dealing within the institution, and you know we are not into that. On top of all that, all our Qurans have been damaged or torn up into pieces, and this is all a violation of the religious act".

Alotta the brothers , been also saying how you've been making shit harder on yourself down here. You're my brother KY, I don't want you to fight a battle that you can't win brotha, especially with these devils. Ain't no winning. We can only control what we can control and leave the rest to Allah.

No matter what they say nor do KY, you got an out date, remember that"! At the moment when I read that I definitely felt what my brother was saying but at the same time, the pride within wanted me to show these devils that I'm just more than 776-361. I'm not state property.

FLOOD THE RANGE WITH MY PAIN

It was chaotic out there. Everyone was either kicking their doors, throwing whatever they can find at correctional officers through the food slot while also flooding the range. This has been happening for the past week, and no one was letting up. A couple of days ago, a correctional officer got waste thrown at him for talking about this guy's mom. Worst part about it is the devils maced the whole block, just for that one incident, and it got everyone heated.

They did an emergency ride out, and shipped dude off to Lukisvile, a level 4 super max. Even though it's been some days after the incident took place, 2 smells were still in the air. The cup of diarrhea dude threw at the C.O. and the mace that still had me sneezing up until this point. There's been a lot of tension on the solitary block as of late, whether it was gang politics, beef with the devils , or people bugging out throwing shit everywhere.

It was a lot to take in, and sleeping wasn't an option especially when everyone was screaming or kicking the cell door. Somehow I was keeping my cool with everything going on. I also still didn't read that page of the Quran I had, which I knew I needed to soon, but I did pray a sunnah (extra prayer) which was a major step in getting the devil out of my ear and was a step closer to getting back on deen.

"FLOOD THE RANGE"!!!

Damn, I rushed quickly to pick up my legal paperwork. Anytime someone decides to flood the range, it just doesn't only piss off the C.O.'s but it affects us, because the water finds its way into your cell. I get up to my door to see what's going on. "AHKI. "

What's niggas flooding the range for"? That shit almost got my legal paperwork soaked." Ahki: Nah brotha, you can't even knock it fr, they ain't been passing out our mail for a minute, and that shit got niggas tight fr"

CELL 8: "C.O I AINT GOING STOP FLOODING THIS SHIT UNTIL I

GET MY MAIL, H** A** N**** A, I got a family mf !".

In all prisons in America, it's considered a federal offense for the institution not to give you your mail. Whether or not they choose to deny it into the facility, they legally must notify you on why they denied your mail. I never really thought too much about getting mail from anyone I loved, not that no one cared about me, but while in solitary or even just being locked up in general, you carry that mentality of "Out of sight out of mind."

That's where I stood at this point, when it came to receiving mail from people in the outside world. If it came through, much love. If not, we live. Is it healthy to think this way? Shiiit, idk, but I know one thing: no one's life will ever stop for mine. Life for your loved ones goes on, while your life here is on pause, that's just the reality.

Red Beard: "INMATES IM LETTING YALL KNOW RIGHT FUCK- ING NOW STOP FLOODING YOUR CELLS. I'M

PASSING OUT MAIL RIGHT NOW, BUT IF I SEE ANYONE FLOODING, I SWEAR I'M SPRAYING THE WHOLE BLOCK." Y'ALL BEEN WARNED A** HOLES".

I shook my head in disbelief. They got this devil working the block. I had one thing in mind, I gotta sleep throughout his whole shift because one thing for sure is that this devil got it out for a nigga. I pace back and forth, zoning out and walking through the puddles of water that filled my cell.

Red Beard: "766-361 HEY YOU FUCKING SOMALI DI** HEAD" "YOU

GOT MAIL." " I yelled back from my tray slot, "Ya man, pass that." He lowered his tone to where I could only hear him. "As a matter of fact, I'm going to read this to make sure it's nothing to do with you selling drugs or getting a phone in here.

I saw the name of the sender as the devil opened it. I bit my lip in anger. "Aye, man stop WTFF; that's a federal crime. You can't open my mail mf"! "Gimme my fucking mail man!" " I swear y'all mf act so tough behind that door, just give me my mail man, you're tripping right now."

Red beard finished reading my mail, and a devilish smile crept up on his face as he spit the chewing tobacco into his cup. Red beard: (low tone voice) " Listen dickhead hope you finally know your place, mf, I know it's you who's sending out messages to other inmates to flood their cells." "Bro, what are you talking about, I ain't tryna talk to you. Just gimme my fuckin mail, you weirdo".

Red beard: Ok, since you want it so bad, see people like you, people like you are meant to be in here, so I'll leave you to it " He threw my mail in my tray slot, then he quickly locked my tray slot". "Aye red beard wtf man, it's hot asf in this bitch, and you gonna lock my only airway?

WTFF." I started kicking the cell door to get his attention, but he was far gone. I started sweating like crazy. I sat on my bed, picked up the letter, and started to read it. What threw me off when Red Beard read my mail was the name of the sender, someone I haven't talked to in years so it was a shock that they reached out.

The letter was sent out months ago, so for me only to get it today shows they were holding our mail. The letter was short and brief..........

After re-reading it for a second time, my heart dropped........

This letter was about my close friend, my brother. He was gone. My face sank into my hands.

My brother was gone from this world, and I didn't know how to take this. He was one of the good ones. No matter the room he entered, his energy and smile was always felt. He brought positivity and love to everyone he's come across. The pain that was forming in my stomach was unbearable.

I wanted to break down, I wanted to cry, I wanted to hug someone, and I wanted to be there for his family. Why did god have to take him so soon & so young? I didn't know how to let my emotions out. All I knew was to turn my pain into anger & rage. Over time as you get older in life, you realize one of the most painful feelings in this world is not a broken nose nor damaged fists, or even a broken leg.

The most painful feeling in this world is seeing the people you made memories with slowly becoming memories. I took my shirt off & wrapped it up in a ball, and pushed it deep into my toilet. Then I started to flush nonstop. I screamed at the top of my lungs as I watched the water rise, as I flooded the cell with my pain.

WITH HARDSHIP COMES EASE

Kick after kick after kick. I wanted the cell door to come off. I was

losing it and had no control of the situation. I wasn't eating much for

the past couple of weeks, and every time C.O's would attempt to put my tray through the slot, I kicked that shit right back out. I was in pain, and this was my mind's only way of coping. I continued to keep kicking the door as hard as I could while also flooding the range.

A Correctional Officer stopped by the cell to observe what was going on. See, this C.O was one of the respectful ones, doesn't come into his shift with an agenda or any disrespect. He puts his hours in and calls it a day. I continued to stomp on the door... C.O: "Aye, aye, aye calm down."

What the hell, what's wrong, man, why are you doing all this? You're making my day harder than it needs to be, and you're making things harder on yourself ". "Man listen, I don't want much. I just need to get in contact with my family and let them know I'm down here man, that's all I ask I promise after that you won't hear nothing from me." I was desperate, and dealing with a lot of pain.

I needed to hear a comforting voice. I needed to hear from my mom and siblings.

C.O: "Even if I tried, man, the block got so much going on all the cell floodings, and I don't know if you heard bout that new virus going on, so ya bud, just be patient and stop kicking your cell door, you do that, and I'll try and get you to talk to your family. Throughout my time, I'd say 97% of the correctional officers you come across are liars and never to be trusted when keeping their word. It was law. Their word just wasn't a guarantee.

With this correctional officer, on the other hand, the chance of him letting me call my family was high. So I calmed down and stopped kicking the door as I watched him walk past my cell. I started to pace back and forth, thinking of the phone call and what I'd talk about with my mom.

I wanted to tell her how much I miss her but just hearing her voice alone would mean everything. I started to get tired of pacing back and forth, and I ended up knocking out on the metal bed. Damn. Hours passing by. I have to get on that phone before the C.O. leaves I moved quickly toward the tray slot to see what was going on.

That's when I heard the keys jangling. Thank God! "Aye, C.O " what's the word "I'm good for that call"? To my shock, I saw the smile of a familiar devil as he continued to swing his keys around. Red beard: phone, haaa hahaha, mother f****, did you forget where the fuck you are?

This is the hole mother f**** and you're an inmate who's in the hole, ain't no f*** phone calls". I never met a human filled with so much hatred & prejudice, towards Black & Muslim people. Red Beard continued to talk shit, as I fought to keep my composure, and that's when he pissed me off for good.

He put his face near my tray slot and whispered the most derogatory words I've heard this devil utter. These words were words that couldn't be repeated, regarding my loved ones. Walahi, I had enough of this devil. From day one, it's almost as if he has one mission, and that's to make my life hell. I called Redbeard to the tray slot.... "Aye red beard".....

Redbeard: "What in the f**** hell do you want inmate. "I told you, no phone calls your in f***** solitary." In a burst of anger, and resentment towards this devil I quickly splashed him with some water from the sink." He yelled in frustration and unlocked my cell, and rushed at me.

I pushed him off me trying to create space. I squared up with him in a defensive stance. The devil quickly grabbed his mace can and aimed it at me as he kept walking closer toward me in this confined space. I had 2 two options; I rush at him and get an extra 3 to 4 years to my sentence, or I can keep dodging the devil, but one thing for sure ain't no dodging mace.

The devil let the whole can off. "AHHHH, I can't breathe". My eyes were choked up and suffering through a burning feeling I had never felt before. My throat felt as if I was suffocating. The devil continued to spray the can as I weakened slowly, bit by bit, and collapsed on the floor. I grabbed the can in an attempt to stop the devil's onslaught.

"Red beard: "Inmate 766-361 has assaulted me, I need back up asap". "You lying devil," I screamed as my throat burned more and more from the mace. Six devils rushed into my cell, and from that point on, all I felt was the pain from the stopping of their combat boots as they all stomped me up.

I started to cover my face and head, which was the only place I could protect myself. In an attempt to break out of this, I tried to stand up, but I already lost a lot of energy from when the devil sprayed his mase can out on me. The stomps continued.

My ribs were on fire, and so was my chest. It started to feel like this was it for a nigga. They continue stomping me out. My vision was getting foggier. I can hear everyone else in solitary kicking their cell doors in frustration. Everyone was supporting me, even at this defeated point I had reached in my life.

That's when I heard Ahki yelling, "Don't fight back, KY, YOU GOT AN OUT DATE." He was right! I have an out date, and I will have a life behind these walls. The devils continued and stomped away and kicked into my torso, but no matter how many times they kicked me I made sure to protect my head.

I knew I could recover from the kicks to my kidneys and my stomach, but I knew I couldn't let these mfs take my mind as well. I wrapped my arms around my skull to continue to protect myself.

The devils continued to stomp me out, and it felt like they weren't stopping anytime soon. Things started to get foggy and all I remember after this was Red Beard approaching me, ready to spray with a new can of mace.

From that point on, my vision was a complete blur. I started to fade away & my mind drifted off to a place.. a nice place, a peaceful place, a place of joy and contentment, a place where I felt like I could run for as long as I wanted, a place where I felt free. No restrictions ,no worries, no pain, no death, no stress.

The burning within my eyes continued, & that peaceful place burned away as well Red beard: "we're done here." All the Devils started walking out

of my cell, then finally slammed the door shut, leaving my legal paperwork thrown all over the floor.

I lay on the cell floor, helpless and defeated. My heart wanted to cry and let all my pain out, but my mind continued to fight against it. My eyes were watered up from all the mace. It's been a long time since I teared up, and I wasn't planning on doing so now. I tried to get up, "Ugh ugggh".

I kept on coughing from all the mace. My ribs were aching. I crawled up and leaned against my metal bed. I was hopeless and had no faith nor hope with what was to come. I started to think about my brother and how his life was taken away too soon. The more I thought of my brother the more my heart started hurting. I couldn't control my rapid breathing.

I started to think about my current circumstance and how these devils had it out for a nigga. I started to think about Ahki's circumstances compared to mine, he's dealing with a life sentence, but yet he's still filled with resilience and hope. He'd always go on about how I needed to read the Quran, and time after time, since being in solitary, I always deflected the importance of what he was talking about. The devil had truly gotten the best out of me.

I continued to lay against the metal bed in defeat and I felt like it was time for me to resort back to the only thing I knew best. Resentment, rage, and bitterness. I looked around in my trashed cell. It looked like Hurricane Katrina had just hit. I looked around at all the legal papers in my cell, a constant reminder of my incarceration, but one page stood out. It was the only page left from my torn up Quran.

I reached for the page and held it up. My disconnect with the most high had reached many different low points. At times I felt like I'd only return to my lord only in those low points. I was nowhere to be found when things got good, but then again, were things ever good?

I tried to stand up, but the burning pain in my body continued. I had trouble breathing, and I wouldn't stop coughing from all the mace. I was mentally and physically broken... With nothing left in me, I finally found some courage to pick up the remaining page of my torn Quran.......

Surah Ash-Sharh 94:1-8

Have We not uplifted your heart for you ˹O Prophet˺, relieved you of the burden

which weighed so heavily on your back, and elevated your renown for you?

So, surely with hardship comes ease.

Surely with ˹that˺ hardship comes ˹more˺ ease.

So once you have fulfilled ˹your duty˺, strive ˹in devotion˺, turning to your Lord ˹alone˺ with hope

I kept on repeating every verse of this chapter. Never have I read anything in depth to the point where each verse started pouring into my soul. I had always resorted to sippin lean during hard times or smoking a backwood, to numb my pain away. I was very familiar with the feeling of pain, but this level of pain felt different. It felt as if the more I read this deep chapter, the more I could heal myself and give me some type of hope, for a better tomorrow.

My mind was moving too fast. Everything was flashing before me.....

Memories of my brother, my dawg, one of the few people who've always kept it real with me.... is no longer on this earth.. I thought of the final time we spoke, and how he was employed, working and telling me that there's a better life for me beyond these bars.....

Thoughts of this confinement, and what was next for me   I thought how

I'm not there to help my brother Abdulahi who's been diagnosed with autism since we were jits......

I thought of my father, wishing he could've been there my whole life, but knowing that wasn't in the cards, even though I still got love for him, the curiosity of a life with him involved floated through my mind.

Then I thought of my life when I'm free. What will I turn out to be? A street nigga that gets buried 6 feet under, or a street nigga that ends up coming back in here, to now doing forever in a day. The purity of this verse made me question everything, but yet it kept letting me know there's hope.

I started to feel my eyes watering up, but it wasn't from the mace. I was crying.. dolo to myself with no one watching but my lord. I cried away and let all the pain, agony, stress, and doubt be released from within. I've never cried throughout my incarceration.

I felt I could always take life head on and desk with everything without showing or having emotion. But in this very moment it was only me and the most high watching so I continued letting my emotions pour away.......

I held the page of the Quran and kept going back to that verse. I continued staring deeply into the verses of this chapter as I wiped away my tears. I kept on reading that same verse.......

So, surely with hardship comes ease. Quran 94:5

PUSH-UPS & DREADLOCKS

Ahki: "88.. 89...90   damn KY, you can never get past 90 push- ups. I know

you can do more than that my nigga." "Aye Ahki, listen bro, for a nigga living off state trays, 90 push-ups per set is pretty good.

Ahki: "Nah my nigga forget all that. You still owe ten more. Don't cheat yourself, treat yourself."

I started laughing as I finished my last push-ups. Every time I neared the finish line, my arms gave up on me.

It's funny because I remember when a nigga could barely do 10 of them. Now I'm out here busting out ten sets of 90s like it's nothing. When it came to doing push- ups, the harder shit got, the more I'd push through.

One of my brothas used to tell me push-ups will push you through life's adversities, and that builds resiliency. Whenever I struggled with a push-up, I'd think of all my adversities, and on top of that, I had Ahki yelling from his cell, motivating me to push through.

It was back on Ahki to knock out his 100 push-ups. We wouldn't know who completed what exact amount of push- ups because we were both in separate solitary cells, but we knew never to cheat the amount because you'd only be selling yourself short. We always kept it a band, regardless of what it was in life. A chess game, a workout, life advice, whatever it was, the brotherhood was authentic. Ahki started his count as he got straight into his push-ups.

Since the beat down, the past months had consisted of me twisting my hair into mini locks, doing push-ups, or reading that verse out of my torn Quran were the only things keeping a nigga going.

My hair length was also the longest it's ever been, and I knew nothing about locks or the history behind them, but somehow as I kept twisting them up, they were finally starting to come together. When it comes to growing hair, it's always been frowned upon in my culture. It's a perception of how you're viewed and how people judge you.

The crazy part is, for a while, I thought it was wrong to have long hair due to how bad Somali culture in America made it seem, to the point the culture would make it seem like it's forbidden in Islam.

Even white American culture has made it a thing to the point they have determined what a professional black person is supposed to look like, which is crazy to me. Let me go back in time real fast. Towards my sentencing date, I knew I was cooked. My lawyer was all about his money and didn't care about me getting convicted.

The state of Ohio had built up enough evidence against me. There was no winning. So as I headed into my sentencing, my lawyer gave me a final visit. He told me I'm doing time regardless, and he said the sentence could be anywhere from 2 to 6 years of prison time.

The devil advised me to cut my hair, and how it can change the judge's heart and opinion of me when he sees me with a low cut, and how also that would give me a "professional look." With me being young and dumb and very trusting in my lawyer, as soon as we were done with the visit, I went straight into my cell and grabbed a razor blade.

I shaved my entire head smooth and bald. I cut my head up a lil bit, but I felt it was all worth it. My smooth bald head started to resemble Kobe. I didn't have dreads at the time, just a mini afro, which was also considered unprofessional, and my family didn't rock with it either.

I headed into the courtroom, and the county jail C.O. rushed me. I was unable to wear my suit for some reason. So instead, I went in there with my inmate jumpsuit shackled from hands to feet.

The judge didn't even look my way. To him, I was just another black inmate in his courtroom, ready to be sent up the road. I got hit with 3 & half, with no county jail time credited & that I was to be shipped to a max security prison.

While he uttered the rest of his closing statements to the courtroom, he still never looked my way. So from then on, it was a simple decision on whether or not to grow out my hair. Who calls the shots on what's professional or not? Why should my character be judged on whether I decide to grow my hair?

I've always believed that people should be considered based on how they conduct themselves, & how they treat their loved ones, and whether or not they stand on morals & principles. These judgmental biases trace back to slavery and systemic racism and currently live on throughout the correctional systems.

When I first got sent up the road, I had to go through reception. This is where they take your blood, DNA, finger prints, height, weight, strip search you, and give you your official inmate number. This is when your prison sentence begins. I remember seeing brothers put through hell just for growing out their hair.

These penitentiaries wanted to strip your pride down completely, and what better way to do so than having niggas cut their hair as soon as they came in through reception. Around this time was a little after my sentencing, so I was still basically bald, and this didn't apply to me then, but everyone else who grew their hair out would have to get it chopped down.

The devils didn't care if you had an afro, twists, or cornrows; they were chopping that shit off. I remember brothers going to solitary for refusing to cut their hair.Some of those brothers were Rastafarian, some were Muslim, some Christian, and some non-religious.All together and united, they stood up and fought for their rights to be themselves & grow out their hair.

About a year after leaving the reception unit to be transferred to my main institution, I came across some brothers who came in from reception. All with different hairstyles that exceeded the "prison hair length rule." I asked them, "Aye bro, they was not chopping niggas hair off at reception?

They responded, saying that after multiple lawsuits and brothers all standing as one and applying the religious act that states; "you can't cut someone's hair off if it's a part of their religion or personal belief". They also told me how state-wide they ended up altogether abolishing this rule, knowing it's a battle even the devils can't win.

Hearing this made me realize, if brothers can work together and unite as one while being behind bars & dealing with oppressors, to fight for what they deserve, what excuse do people on the outside world have not to be able to do the same while granted their freedoms?

One thing that's also sad is how folks lost their culture and their pride within, & have taken after Eurocentric beauty standards. Still, folks need to stop judging people who decide not to follow those standards & decide to grow their hair out.

This level of judgment is pretty corny if you ask me. Growing up, I never really had too much hair. My mom always made me keep my hair short, but I had a homie who always grew his hair out, but in doing so, he took a lot of criticism for it from within the community.

What's crazy is he's good people, never committed crimes, ain't do anyone bad, ain't smoke, never drank none of that. All he did was grow his hair out. The community always had a perception that homie was a drug dealer or did drugs (by the way, we were only 13 years old at the time), and due to the constant perception and negativity & pressure that was held over his head, it led him to cut his hair. The opinions of others shouldn't ever dictate one's reasoning for cutting their hair.

I made a promise to myself after my sentencing date, when I decided to go bald, hoping to impress a judge into thinking I'm a better black man with a low cut. You see, that's where I messed up, and I promised myself from that day on to never switch up my appearance or what I stand for, to be accepted or respected by individuals that don't approve of who I am, from that day on... I was me.....

I finally finished retwisting my locs. I counted each lock from all sides of my head, ensuring everything looked even and crisp. It was starting to come along for me, and I was rocking with it. Ahki: Ayeee K.Y, what's taking you so long bro"? It's back on you, and push yo self bro"!

"No excuses my brotha get to that hun-dun"! Ahki was right! No more excuses. No more giving up. I had started something, but my thoughts of saying "I can't do it," stopped me from seeing that finish line. "Ahki, let's get it. I'm getting to that hundred"!!! I kept pushing myself "20.... "35.... 48.... 55....60... 79....

85..".

My arms tightened up, and my chest was burning. I had 15 more push-ups to go. With every push-up, I was 1 step closer to smacking my face on the floor. "91"....

I was on my final nine push-ups, and I swear to god, I didn't know how else to push myself to knock out the last 9... then it hit me, I remembered all the obstacles I've pushed through, not having my pops around, growing up to dealing with the deaths of loved ones, to being incarcerated at 18 years old, and sent to a max, to be then jumped by multiple C.O's while thrown in solitary...

I was young, but I've seen a lifetime of some shit... "95". Ahki: come on KY, push yourself my nigga, get through this. You got 5 to go my brother, push through". I started to count from 5 down.

"FIVE"; Push through for the homies who ain't on this earth. ..

"FOUR"; Push through for the homies serving forever in a day...
"THREE"; Push through for everything I put my mom through...

"TWO"; Push through for all those lonely, defeated nights when you felt you had no one by your side

"ONE"; !!!!!! Ima always push through because Allah hasn't given up on me. The most high keeps giving me the resilience to keep on going, and that's exactly what ima do.

I heard Ahki laughing in the background. He was happy that I finally completed a full rep of 100 push-ups, but I had much more work to do. I got ready for the next set of hundreds.

I finally understood that I have to persevere and push through regardless, and be ready to empower myself, no matter the difficulties I face.

COVID, BROTHERHOOD, & PRAYER

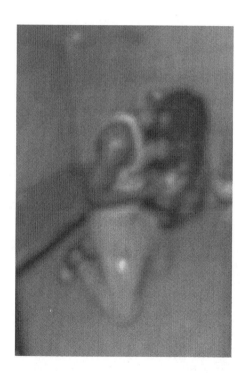

I turned on my sink to start my day. I started washing my face, and surprisingly, my water went brown again. This was something I had gotten used to, to the point I even knew how to take away the brown water temporarily. I turned on my sink and turned it back on in a minute, and just like it always does, my sink's water turned clear once again.

I started to make wudu (prayer cleansing); I started by washing my face and felt facial hair underneath my chin, something I've never had. I'd be lying if I said feeling my lil chin hair didn't have me geeked up about it. The thought of growing up, and now I am laughing to myself about all this chin hair.

I wrapped up my wudu by washing up my right & left foot 3 times each. I stood tall & firm ready to begin prayer. Once ending prayer, I made my supplications & sat on my cell floor in silence. A new habit I had picked up since being in confinement. I was amazed at how much peace this would put me at.

Peace of mind was something I wasn't accustomed to. For me, peace was one of those things that was lost in childhood, lost for a very long time. I sat longer after prayer thinking about the past couple of months and how downhill everything's been, thoughts of my homie, my close brother who passed. I always kept him in my prayers, and my bro always wanted what was best for me, so I'm forever praying that god allows us to reunite again in paradise. I've always wondered, for all my wrongdoings in life, does the good I've done outweigh the bad.

I knew one thing fosho, the Imam of the prison, would always remind me that Allah is the most forgiving, and no matter how bad you do if you turn to him, he got you fosho. I got up off the cell floor and started stretching. It was that time. I clenched up my fists and knocked out some fist push-ups. I kept going until failure. I aimed to see if I could knock out more than 100 straight, and I had no intention of disappointing myself. I kept pushing through, my knuckles were starting to give up on me, but I kept on going.

I found a different way to tame my anger, pain, and life losses, through push-ups and prayer. Finally! I'm at 80. I had to pass 100; ain't no slowing down. Sounds of jangling keys were nearing my cell....C.O: "Africa, you haven't been on your loud ass sh** lately, huh? "That beat down, did you right." I continued my push-ups, ignoring the devil, something I'd never done before. I've gotten accustomed to the habit of them barking at me, and my go-to is to bark right back, but this time was different.

I was locked in, and I truly felt there was nothing the devil could do to affect the mental state I'd entered. He kept on talking his head off for a little bit longer, then realized there was no response coming his way. The devil finally left, and I heard his keys jingling farther away.

By the time I knew it, I had broken a record. I had finally reached 130 push-ups straight! "Ahkiiiii" I yelled out my cell in excitement; I was breathing so heavily, trying to catch my breath. "Ahkiiiii, aye man, I did that shit, man I did that shit, man 130 straight, Ahki, 130 straight"!

Ahki: I told you, you got it, man; the only person that can stop KY is KY, & my nigga, don't forget about salat too". Ahki; "In a minute". "I responded

with the same words as I moved away from my cell door. (We'd always "say in a minute" as our way to disperse after a conversation took place)I took in the words Ahk told me....

For a long time, I constantly doubted myself. Always thinking that I'm a no-good nigga, a failure. Things were looking up. I started to think beyond these cell walls, and I started to look at things in life from a different angle. Instead of counting down days in this cell, I started seeking knowledge in all aspects of life.

Whether it was something simple as praying all five prayers, I'd write it on the wall, or whenever Ahki would yell about crypto and how it's changing the outside world, I'd write it on the wall. I had no pencil sharpener, but I had made it a habit not to bite my nails so they could grow into a pencil sharpener.

I'd also write down different workouts Ahki would tell me about, such as slower variations of push-ups and jumping jacks. I turned my cell into a knowledge bubble; whatever ideas popped up in my head,

I'd write down on the wall. I used to think the people that were real in my life were those who put me in a position to make bread and elevate in the game.

In all reality, these same niggas could care less. The moment you get caught up trying to make that money they no longer know you. It shows you that these friendships hold no value and aren't authentic, ain't shit real. I remember cutting ties with all knowledgeable genuine people who actually gave an f about my well-being. Living in this street life comes with a cost: everything that's real goes down the drain. Real friendships, real peace of mind, good health, and true happiness all go down the drain.

All my so-called niggas disappeared on me. I only had five people out of the 20 to 30 folks I'd kick with thinking they were some "real niggas", but what even made them real? All because of what? The fact we made money together. One thing Ahki would always tell me about is that a real friend, or a "real nigga" doesn't put you in harm's way but passes you the tools to elevate in life without coming across jail or death.

The thing about my bro Ahki is no matter the circumstance or where we were, solitary confinement or the general popula- tion, he'd always advise me and put me on the game of legit opportunities that won't land me back in prison when I made it home.

Even behind bars, Ahki was so in tune with the word. He'd always read the WSJ front to back, then pass it out to his closest brothers and let us know the main articles to read up on. Just a couple of days ago he was talking to me about the benefits of franchising a well-known company compared to starting up your own business.

He explained everything from the taxes, to the percentages of profit that can be made to also explaining what needs to be invested into a franchise and what it takes for you to grow within that franchise. & also opening up multiple franchises & the benefits that go into that. Every time I spoke with Ahki I turned into a sponge.

The thing about Ahki is he didn't talk to a lot of people. Stand up guy. He'd pray, call his family, work out, and read books, but books that carried knowledge. He'd always tell me to avoid fiction books and books that don't improve my growth. He always told me to read history books, autobiographies/biographies on accomplished people, & self-growth books as well.

My whole life, I had a way of describing a real nigga, a brother. Someone who always is ready when shit pops off, someone who puts me onto all the fast money routes, someone who's always with his brother for all pop-outs, all the club t'ups, all of that.

That's who I considered "my brothers, "my real niggas." In all reality, I pushed away all my good friends a long time ago when I dove deeper into this lifestyle. So now, in my current situation, I know to see the things for what they are, not for what I want them to be.......

I laid it down on my metal bed; I started feeling fatigued, and a minor headache started to kick in. I don't what kicked this headache in but I know it had to be them push-ups, a nigga pushed himself to the limits.

I started to doze off, knowing a deep sleep awaited; for a long time, I hadn't had a dream of peace and full happiness. No stress & no problems involved. I either saw darkness. Or I either had nightmares. All praise to the most-high. Ever since I started praying my daily 5, the nightmares would disappear.

I was still yet to have a good dream, but I found peace within daydreaming. Before I'd go to sleep, I'd picture myself in a suit. I never owned a suit, but I wondered how clean it would look.

I'd always picture a professional version of me. The future older version of myself, a free man. No restraints, no pain, no suffering, just a free KY who's at peace.

I continued to visualize this and finally went into a deep sleep.Damn what the hell. I woke up feeling like I had a crazy hangover, and the throbbing in my head was unbearable. The headaches made me feel I could possibly pass out. I felt as if I was on my deathbed. I got off the metal bed to see a puddle of sweat all over the place and sweat all over my body.

I felt wind chills kick in. It felt like it was going to snow. I put my hand on my forehead and immediately knew I had a fever. I never really had a fever since being locked up & in general, I never had fevers when I was free, but this one felt different. My breathing felt very limited. Every breath I took felt restrained. This experience was different. Days started to fly by and the symptoms worsened. The toll this was taking on my body was something I never experienced before.

I physically was so weak, & and a nigga hadn't eaten in days. The lack of fresh air and natural light didn't help either. The once muscular frame that I had built up had settled down into all bones. This grasp of this virus tightened its hold on my mind as well. I thought of yelling for a C.O. so I could go to the infirmary and get some medicine, but knowing how these devils operate, the chances of that happening were slim, but what other options did I have? A nigga dying in here.

"C.O" I yelled as loud as I could. No response. My voice started to crack and I started to feel heavy chest pains. I looked under my cell door to see the boots of a herd of correctional officers. I could barely hear due to the fact they were all talking in multiple conversations, but there was one main thing I was able to catch on to.

A couple of the C.O's spoke about the number of people they had in intake and how the hole was over-capacitated. They kept speaking on this new virus tearing the world up and how the institutions are understaffed and will have to call the national guard in to monitor the prison.

I couldn't catch the virus name, but I heard the devils speaking on behalf of the symptoms. Chest pains, difficulties in breathing and fever, and major fatigue were all symptoms I was currently dealing with.

I yelled out from the seam of the cell door:" Aye, C.O, I got that virus y'all talking about." Again no response. I was beginning to get frustrated with dealing with this unknown Alotta mysterious shit was going on outside my cell. Guys were getting rushed out of their cells in the middle of the night on stretchers.

People were coughing and sneezing all day, and a limited number of correctional officers were watching over the solitary block. What was also weird was that the worry amongst C.O's about this new virus had them shaking out their boots.

I also haven't heard from Ahk in a few days, and my symptoms weren't doing me justice. I began to pace back and forth, and I stood in front of the steel toilet as I looked into my reflection. My eyes were weary. My face looked as if it had been stripped from its natural appeal. I was going through a health crisis I've never experienced before.

I wanted to pray and get close to my lord, but in an attempt to do prayer cleansing, I threw up all over the sink. A niggas chest was on fire, and my stomach was wrapped up into a knot of pain. With no medical help, nor proper nutrition, I laid down and made supplication for Allah to take this pain away.

I kept shivering as I made my way to my rack, and after that, shit……..

Everything was a blur.

C.O: "CELL 4" "CELL 4" (HEAVY KICKING AT THE DOOR) The kicksto my door had me up in a hurry. I looked at my metal rack to see the huge puddle of sweat I was fully drenched in. How long have I been out for ?

I felt my stomach rumble, and it was like he was sending me a message letting me know it could eat food now. I still had headaches and was shivering, but I felt the fever calm down.

C.O: "CELL 4 this my last time asking you", you have a religious book from Cell 5". I immediately got up. On my way to the cell door, my head felt as if it got hit by a boulder. I made my way to the door, and the C.O passed the religious book from under the cell door. The book title said "the autobiography of Malcolm X."

It wasn't a religious book, but I knew I had a good read ahead of me about an inspirational human being that I had always looked up to in my early childhood days.

Growing up, when living on the Westside of Columbus in river point, my mom wasn't a fan of cable, and it's not like niggas grew up on iPads. It was either play outside, go to the Rp courts, and watch the older guys hoop while you ride your scooter or bike down the hill of the neighborhood. I did all that growing up but I found myself reading a lot of books as well.

One of the main books I read was about Malcolm, the trials and tribulations that he overcame during his lifetime. Malcolm went from being a man with no faith, no structure, and no discipline to be one of the greatest leaders our world has seen. He had a backbone, stood for something, and lived by it. I quickly dove into the autobiography despite still feeling fever symptoms. I knew how important of a read this was due to how important Malcolm was for me growing up....

I continued reading, and was into the autobiography. By the time I knew it I was already 4 chapters in. I flipped to the next page and saw a note that was folded up into a very small triangle that was wrapped up with string to help seal the note. I opened it up, it was from Ahki.....

Note from Ahki: As salaam alaikum (peace be upon you) "KY man the world out here spooked about this virus called COVID- 19. I just got over it after being hospitalized for the past week. When I tell you this shit is a pandemic bro, it's bad, bro wallahi. C.O. 's getting sick, and missing out work, at least 20 inmates are being transferred to the ER, and they are also saying some folks passed away from the virus.

So ya bro it's crazy, it's even worse on the street. It just recently hit the prisons, but this shii been going on for months now. It got the outside world in shambles. Everyone is scared out here bro.

As the numbers go up, the virus continues to have all the higher ups shook. These shaytans (devils) are all struggling to contain the outbreak and keep the number of deaths from the virus under wraps; you have families calling in the institution and aren't able to tap in with their people.

In an attempt to control the situation, the higher ups made a controversial decision: they decided to put all the inmates with

COVID-19, including those who were asymptomatic, in solitary confinement.

What's crazy KY, is even with this decision made by the institution, it's not like they are testing anyone for having Covid-19. I'm also hearing that the national guard has been called up to help run the institution since all the C.O's been calling off sick. I don't know if you caught covid or not, but I know one thing: you must stay active. Do some jumping jacks, and I promise it'll help you sweat it out.

This an older man's sickness brother this ain't nothin to a champ; you gotta sweat that shii out, but check this though brotha. I'm getting sent up to max security up in Toledo, and the bus rides out first thing early tomorrow morning. Here goes my moms number and my cousin's numbers too. I also left my inmate number for you on the back of this letter. You are a smart guy brother and you got Allah by your side. It's crazy, bro; it feels like yesterday when I calculated the hours you had to do in total, what was it?

Yup, 30,660 hours. I remember your face, bro, you looked like you were going to pass out, and now they got you doing solitary time on top of that. Remember this bro, Allah puts his toughest soldiers through the toughest battles. You're a tough soldier bro you gonna do this time and come out better!

That's why I told you the exact hours of your sentence so you can learn from it, but shii man love you my brother and definitely keep in contact. We're locked in. You're going to do some great things out there, and last but not least nigga......

"DON'T FORGET TO PRAY". pray for yourself, your family and those you lost in this life. peace brotha, one love. Assalaamu alaikum."

(Peace and blessings be upon you)

I finished reading the note and realized my eyes started to water up. I wanted to contain the tears, but I had no control. The tears began to pour down my face, but this felt different. These weren't tears of pain. These were tears of appreciation. I appreciated that I had a brother who motivated me to do good.

I was appreciative to know I had a brother who wanted to see me win in life without having to ever jeopardize my livelihood and freedom. I was appreciative that I had a brother that wanted me to be closer to god. I appreciated my brother Ahki and all my brothers, which motivated me toward good.

I finally understood what true brotherhood is all about.

I wiped the tears off my face, and I looked up on my cell walls, a whole bunch of knowledge I wrote down passed down all from Ahki.

I got up off my bed and took my brother's advice as always. I got up and began my prayer. "As salamu alaikum wa rahmatullahi wa barakatuh " (Peace be upon you and God's mercy and blessings.) I concluded my prayer, and sat in pure silence....

For a long time, I only looked at the bad and never profoundly looked into the blessings god has bestowed upon me. I got up and got straight into a set of jumping jacks, I was all the way locked in. With a strong foundation of faith, a strong will, and an understanding of true brotherhood is all about. I knew I had more than what it takes to get over COVID-19.

OPEN UP CELL 4

I layed in a deep sleep. It wasn't a comfortable deep sleep, but it was sleep, and when you can attain that, it's your escape from hell. I started to twist and turn. I kept on hearing different sounds.

The sounds I was hearing were sounds I'd grown accustomed to. The sounds of jingling keys and the heavy footsteps of multiple devils echoed down the hallway, & there went my sleep. But sleeping wasn't on my mind. My focus was on today, a day I had eagerly been anticipating.

The 90 days of solitary had finally come to an end, and I would be transferred to a maximum-security prison. The sounds of C.O. Red Beard's devilish voice filled the air as he unlocked my cell, letting me know it was time to pack it up.

"Pack it up, Africa." Your time's up," he barked; his hatred for me was written all over his arrogant smirk. Cuffing me up, he prepared me for the journey ahead, his words dripping with contempt. Red Beard never missed an opportunity to remind me of his belief that I would end up right back in prison, back into solitary confinement, and how I had a life of misery and failures ahead of me.

His negativity always could get under my skin, provoking me to respond aggressively. But now, with the newfound strength I gained through faith, discipline, & brotherhood, I could laugh off his words.

They held no value or weight to ever throw me off my hookup. I actually started looking at Red Beard as a motivation. By striving against his beliefs of me never amounting to anything, I knew I'd prove him wrong and myself right... That I can be something.

As Red Beard finished securing the handcuffs, I took a moment to reflect on how much I had transformed during my time in solitary. The old me would have succumbed to anger and resentment, but through the walls of my cell, I filled my mind with knowledge and hope for a better tomorrow.

I wrote down the names of all my loved ones who had passed away, creating a memorial on the walls of my confinement. I also thought of my brother, friend, and brother for life, Ahki. He always put me on game and I'm forever grateful for that.

Staring at the cell walls, I couldn't help but notice how much I had aged mentally, but in a positive way. Scratching my goatee, a feature I never had. I was shaken up by the growth I had experienced.

My dreadlocks also reached new heights, a testament to the passage of time and my personal transformation. My confinement had become a catalyst for my personal growth, forcing me to confront my demons head-on and emerge as a stronger person on the other side.

As the heavy metal door to my solitary confinement cell finally slid open, I couldn't believe my ears. The cheers and shouts of encouragement filled the air, echoing through each cell in the pod. The sounds of the homies' voices reached my ears, reminding me that I was not alone in this dark place.

"KY! You made it, brother! I told you they can't hold you down forever!" yelled one of my close Muslim brothers, Mo, his voice carrying the weight of all the years spent behind these cold, unforgiving walls.

The energy in the air was electrifying. The love was real. Every cell I passed, every face I saw, was an ally or a comrade. There was an outpouring of support. Homies from all walks of life stood in front of their cells with fists raised in unity.

"Stay strong, KY & keep ya head high!" shouted Santos, one of the Hispanic homies whose ink told stories of its own. I nodded and smiled, my heart grateful for the love and unity that flowed through these walls.

Their words fueled my determination, reminding me that I was not just an individual but part of a brotherhood that stretched beyond the confinement of this hell hole. Red Beard was annoyed by the love. He muttered under his breath; the devil hated seeing the love & support pouring out for the kid. "All you mf, shut the f*** up!" Red Beard was pissed.

His voice echoed through the halls of solitary. But his words only seemed to ignite the cheers & support even louder. "KY! You're gonna make it, lil bro"! You made it through this. I promise nothing will stop you!" The encouragement from Razaq was felt, a wise old man I had my fair share of chess battles with, who had found peace within Islam during his time behind these walls. Red Beard grew more pissed with each passing cell, and his face turned into a tomato.

His face was filled with anger and frustration. But despite all attempts to silence the support, the voices of the voiceless continued to rise. It didn't matter what gang you were in or what faith you believed in. In this very moment, we were all united, standing as one, pushing against the darkness that sought to consume us. As I finally reached the end of the solitary unit, the kicking of the cell doors and cheers had ended. I stopped and faced the rows of cells within the solitary unit.

I turned back and punched my fist into my chest, symbolizing gratitude and defiance. "Thank you, my brothers"! I'll never forget any of y'all walahi! We Konnected for life!" I shouted as loud as possible. Red beard aggressively grabbed me by my shackles, he was tired of me, and for the first time ever, the devil looked defeated as we walked towards the exit. Red Beard opened the exit door, and we walked towards the bus.

My eyes kept on squinting against the blinding sunlight. It was the first time in 90 days that I had seen the sun. A nigga felt like a vampire. I was shaken up by the intensity of the rays of light.

As I continued to slowly regain my steps, my vision adjusted to the brightness of God's creation. Even though I was headed to another max prison of 23 and 1, I was geeking for the minor freedoms that awaited me. Being able to call my family & loved ones after all this time was the only thing on my mind.

The journey to the new maximum-security prison was annoying as hell. The bus ride was already uncomfortable with the bumpy journey; the trip was only made worse by being shackled with another inmate.

But I didn't let it affect my spirits. Instead, I seized the opportunity to reflect on the trials and tribulations I had faced throughout my lifetime. As I looked out of the bars of the tinted windows on the prison bus, I watched all the cars pass by in a blur.

Painful memories flooded my mind. I recalled the countless battles I had to go against. Constant hatred and systemic racism from the devils, all while dealing with the unbearable pain of my friend's death.

In those 90 days of solitude, I had finally learned to seek out the light, even when the tunnel seemed so dark. I had complete trust in Allah that the future would be full of promise, with a bright path ahead, regardless of the hardships that awaited. With each passing moment, my resilience grew, along with my confidence.

Now I knew no matter what challenges lay ahead, as long as I stayed true to who I am and what I stand for, I'd always prevail. The journey to another maximum security prison would be just another chapter in my life, & another opportunity to overcome adversity and become more vital than ever before. As the bus rumbled, I held onto the lessons I had learned in solitary. I was no longer defined by my circumstances; nothing could stop me.

A LETTER TO KY

I hope & pray that this letter makes it to the institution; I already know how they are with the mail. I really hope you take the time to read this because, I really love you bro…..

Trust me when I say I understand everything you're going through. I know you are dealing with a lot of pain, bitterness, and rage right now, and it may feel like there is no hope for the future. But I want you to know that there is always hope.

No matter how dark things may seem, there is always a light at the end of the tunnel. It's gonna take some time to get there, and the road will be rocky and difficult, but you, of all people, can do it. I want you to know that you are not alone in your struggles. People care about you and want to see you succeed. Even if you don't feel like you have a lot of people in your corner right now, know that one day, you'll come across people, good people, that care for you and want to see you grow and be better than you were yesterday.

Also, KY, I know a lot of people have written you off and view you as a criminal who's serving 3 and a half years, but don't ever let the judgment of others dictate who you become as a person. Always remember this lil bro, no matter what happens, life will continue, and your loved ones' lives will go on as well.

Still, there's one person whose everyday livelihood is deprived and pained by your incarceration. Lil bro, this is the only person who cried herself to sleep every night when thinking about you. She was there, from the school suspensions to the juvenile courts to your adult imprisonment, yet she has still not given up on you. Her love for you is pure, lil bro.

This person I speak of is your beautiful, caring, and loving mother, and if you are not willing to change your life, it is a disservice to the love this woman has for you. So you gotta do better by her. Hooyo (mom) loves you, man, and wants the best for you, and seeing you incarcerated is definitely taking a toll on her mentally and emotionally.

But remember that change takes time, and you can't let the guilt of hurting your mother hold you back from making positive changes. Use her love and support as motivation to turn your life around and become the person she knows you can be. Hoyo's love is unconditional, and she will always be there for you. But you owe it to her and yourself to become the best version of yourself, and anything less of that lil bro shouldn't be an option.

Please, bro, while you are in there, up your skills and knowledge on life, whether it's understanding the law of this country, playing chess, reading books, praying, and working out, so when you touch down, you'll have what it takes to build a better future for yourself.

There are a lot of pointless conversations in prison, & on the outside world that glamorize the lifestyle you took part in. Knowing you, bro, you're struggling between steering clear or jumping back into that lifestyle. I'm letting you know right now, KY, it's not worth it. There's no winning in this lifestyle.

The odds are stacked against you bro. You are a young Muslim Black Somali man in America who has racked up 3 felonies with a juvenile record. So if I'm being real with you, the odds aren't in your favor, especially when doing anything that can cause you to do more time. So why jeopardize your freedom once again?

Fam, is it really worth making some quick cheese? The same quick cheese that caged you up for 30,660 hours of your life? The quickness that cheese comes into your pockets is as quick as it'll disappear. Fast money doesn't last, KY. All the designer brands you were rocking, now you're in the pen wearing state blues with 6 digits on your shirt.

You see the pain this life has brought you and your loved ones. There's so much opportunity out here, lil KY; you just gotta take it. There's a world out here that you neglected to look at. There are opportunities to make a great living without risking your freedom ever again.

I know how appealing fast money is, but that slow money will stick longer. I promise KY, I forget it's crazy you've never seen a beach, palm trees, or even made (hajj) pilgrimage. I'm telling you there's more to life than catching plays and taking risks, all that to lose years of life. That's not living, lil bro. I want you to see the world, a world that this lifestyle has robbed you of.

Making the change won't be easy, but with hard work, discipline, and determination, wallahi, you can make a positive change in your life and in the lives of those who love you. Ky, I want to remind you that you are more than your mistakes. Your past does not define you; think of all the homies rooting for you to make it.

Alotta the homies don't get a second chance at the apple. You've seen so many of your loved ones lose their life, or lose it to the system. Don't give up, bro... don't give up.

There's a quote that will resonate with you more so than anyone;

"Y'all can shackle my arms and legs, throw me in a box, but y'all can never take my mind." I know that you have the strength and resilience to overcome this adversity.

Keep your head up, and know that there is always hope, and never let the oppressors take that hope away from you. Stay focused; your future needs you, lil bro. & remember that your time there is temporary; you got an out date. You have a future beyond your current situation.

Take this one day at a time. You are only 18 & I know the time is overwhelming, but you will walk through the storm and come out of it a million times stronger. God only puts his toughest soldiers through the toughest of battles.

KY, I know how you feel. I know you feel betrayed by those you loved & trusted, but hatred is not the way to go. I promise you lil bro, no good will come from it. You're young with a bright future ahead, but that future can only happen once you release the hate from within.

You can't live like that, lil bro; I promise it won't take you far. I understand how it is to feel hurt and betrayed by those you put your love and trust in, but holding onto anger and hatred towards them will only harm you in the long run lil KY.

You gotta learn to forgive those who have wronged you and focus on moving forward with a positive outlook. You earned the name KY (Konnected Youngin) for a reason, and you gotta hold up to it, lil bro.

You have connected with people from different backgrounds and different parts of the globe, who have all put you on game since a youngin. So it is a slap in the face to keep that same mentality for all those great people who passed on knowledge to see you grow. Lil KY, you control your own life, and you have the power to create your own destiny.

Don't let the corrections system, judgment of others, and life's circumstances ever hold you back from pursuing your dreams and living the life you want to live. Always show love no matter what lil bro. I know pops wasn't a major part of your life but don't allow that to dictate where you stand with him today. Always show him love and respect, no matter what, because he's your pops, and no matter the circumstances that life has given you, you gotta always show love.

No one's perfect, & sometimes most show love in different ways; you just gotta accept that and continue being a positive human being. Also, fix your relationships with your sibling's lil bro. Your sentence has also been painful for them all, and some have different ways of showing that pain, but you gotta be patient and be the best brother you can be to them all.

You just gotta let 'em know that y'all will make it through this storm & that you'll be the best brother you can be for them through it all & a better brother when it's all over. KY, no matter what lil bro, continue elevating in all aspects of life, day by day, hour by hour, minute by minute because life's short my nigga, and nothing in this world is guaranteed.

Be grateful that Allah has protected you through everything. Allah could've easily put you 6 feet under, but he chose this as your trajectory. And definitely stay on course with your workouts; I know how that shit keeps you sane and disciplined. Finally, KY, no matter how difficult the road may seem, I promise you lil bro, there is always hope at the end of it.

By facing your everyday adversities and hardships head-on, you will become stronger, more disciplined, more resilient, and better equipped to handle whatever challenges are thrown your way. Keep moving forward, and just know before anything that with belief in Allah, perseverance, and a positive outlook on life, anything is possible my nigga....you're going to make it KY.....

I promise......

Sincerely from someone who truly loves you,

........Yourself

ABOUT THE AUTHOR

Yusuf Ahmed, but better known as K.Y. A first generation Somali who was raised in the city of Columbus, Ohio. He has triumphed over numerous challenges in his life. His personal journey of overcoming adversity has shaped him into a source of empowerment, inspiration, and motivation for others. Throughout the years his experiences has brought him to understand that one's obstacles and past do not define them, but rather serve as catalysts for growth and transformation. Motivated by his past struggles & adversities,

K.Y has dedicated his life to empowering individuals who've dealt with hardships, & is on a mission to make a positive impact on his community and society as a whole. He founded The E.T.A Foundation (EMPOWERMENT THROUGH ADVERSITY) and uses that as a means to fulfill his mission.

The foundation focuses on providing support and guidance to those who are currently incarcerated within the prison system, as well as mentoring the youth to prevent them from ending up behind bars. The author believes in the power of education, rehabilitation, and mentorship as essential components for creating a better future. He engages with individuals who have been affected by the criminal justice system, offering them guidance and support to help them reintegrate into society successfully. By advocating for more opportunities for those with felonies, K.Y aims to break down barriers and create a more inclusive world.

K.Y is also a practicing Muslim and takes a lot of pride in his faith. This helped shape out his principles, guidelines, & discipline, that he continues to work on till this day. The author is just like you, a son to his mother, a brother to his many siblings, and a member of his community. He has a love for the game of basketball, but has a major passion for fitness as a whole, since it empowered him through the darkest of times. Through his writing, he shares his story, shedding light on the struggles he has overcome and offering valuable insights for others navigating their own challenges. His words resonate with the youth, encouraging them, and letting them know to embrace their inner strengths, rewrite their narratives, and pursue a life of purpose. With compassion and determination, the author continues to touch lives and build a legacy that transcends boundaries, proving that one person's journey can ignite a spark of hope and change the world for the better.